DATE DUE

AG 25 '99		
MR 20 '00		
SE 28 '02		
JY _ 1 '03		
JY - 7 '03		
JY 21 '03		

CLINTON TOWNSHIP
Public Library
Waterman, Illinois

1. Books may be kept two weeks and may be renewed once for the same period, except 7 day books and magazines.
2. A fine is charged for each day a book is not returned according to the above rule. No book will be issued to any person incurring such a fine until it has been paid.
3. All injuries to books beyond reasonable wear and all losses shall be made good to the satisfaction of the Librarian.
4. Each borrower is held responsible for all books charged on his card and for all fines accruing on the same.

21246   DEMCO

Military Trucks

by Michael Green

Reading Consultant:

Sergeant James Petersen (retired)

United States Air Force

C A P S T O N E   P R E S S

M A N K A T O ,   M I N N E S O T A

C A P S T O N E   P R E S S

818 North Willow Street • Mankato, Minnesota 56001

Printed in the United States of America.

Library of Congress Cataloging-in-Publication Data
Green, Michael (Michael R.)
    Military trucks/by Michael Green.
    p. cm. — (Land and sea)
    Includes bibliographical references and index.
    Summary: Discusses the history and use of military trucks, highlighting specific models and their roles in various battles.
    ISBN 1-56065-463-5
    1. Military trucks—United States—Juvenile literature. 2. United States Army—Transportation—Juvenile literature. [1. Military trucks. 2. Trucks.] I. Title. II. Series: Land and sea (Mankato, Minn.)
UG618.G75 1997
823.7'47—dc21

                        96-39035
                          CIP
                            AC

Photo credits
AM General: 4, 8, 28, 36, 38. FMC: 17, 18
William B. Folsom: 12, 34, 47. Michael Green: 6, 26
Oshkosh Truck Company: 30, 33
Stewart Stevenson Services: 41. U.S. Army: 10, 14, 22, 24
Visuals Unlimited/Arthur R. Hill: 20

Table of Contents

Chapter 1 Military Trucks 5

Chapter 2 World War II U.S. Army Trucks ... 11

Chapter 3 Special U.S. Army Trucks 21

Chapter 4 Postwar U.S. Army Trucks 27

Chapter 5 Safer Army Trucks 35

Features

Historical Map 18

Photo Diagram 36

Words to Know 42

To Learn More 44

Useful Addresses 45

Internet Sites 46

Index 48

Pronunciation guides follow difficult words, both in the text and in the Words to Know section in the back of the book.

Chapter 1

Military Trucks

Military trucks have an important job. They deliver the supplies an army needs to fight and survive. Military trucks bring food, fuel, and ammunition to soldiers.

Military trucks never receive credit for winning a battle or a war. But they are the silent heroes of any successful army. Armies would be not be able to win battles or wars without sturdy, dependable trucks.

Tough and Rugged

Military trucks come in many sizes. Different trucks have different jobs. Small trucks can go where big trucks cannot. But big trucks can

Military trucks can drive through almost anything.

carry things small trucks cannot. A division of 15,000 soldiers needs more than 2,000 trucks to keep it supplied.

Military trucks have to be tough to last in combat. They are driven where there are no roads. Sometimes soldiers are too busy to take care of their trucks. The trucks have to keep running without regular maintenance.

Military trucks are often the targets of enemy fire. The enemy knows that the supplies carried by the trucks are important.

This military truck is a 6x6. All of its wheels are powered.

Wheels and Power

Some military trucks have as many as 12 wheels. Not all the wheels on military trucks are powered. Only powered wheels are counted. If a truck has 12 wheels but only six of them are powered, it is called a 6x6 (six-by-six) truck.

The powerful M939 can go through deep water.

A large military truck may be a 6x6 or an 8x8. Trucks with more wheels are less likely to become stuck in soft ground.

The U.S. Army Jeep is a small 4x4 truck. All four of a Jeep's wheels have power supplied to them. The Jeep is also made for civilians. Civilian means they are not used by the military.

Civilian trucks are the kind regular people buy at car and truck dealers to use every day. Civilian trucks do not have to cross soft ground with heavy loads. They do not need as many wheels. Most off-road civilian trucks are 4x4s.

Cargo and Weight

Military trucks are also known by the amount of cargo the truck was made to carry. The U.S. Army has two-and-one-half-ton (2.25-metric-ton) trucks and five-ton (4.5-metric-ton) trucks.

The amount of cargo a military truck can actually carry depends on road conditions. A five-ton (4.5-metric-ton) truck might not be able to carry five tons (4.5 metric tons) of cargo in soft sand. But on a highway, the same five-ton (4.5-metric-ton) truck might be able to carry 10 tons (nine metric tons) of cargo.

The Jeep

The prototype for the Jeep was known as the General Purpose vehicle. This was soon abbreviated to just GP. People said "GP" like it was a word. It sounded like "Jeep".

The Willys-Overland company made the Jeep prototype. Willys-Overland liked the name, and that is how this 4x4 became known as a Jeep.

Chapter 2

World War II U.S. Army Trucks

Companies in the United States built more than 3 million military trucks for use in World War II (1939-1945). Most were built for the U.S. Army. Many were also used by the U.S. Marine Corps (KOHR).

The Jeep

The most famous U.S. Army truck during World War II was the Jeep. The Jeep was a light truck. It weighed about one ton (one metric ton).

World War II soldiers depended on their rugged trucks.

The wartime Jeep was 11 feet (three meters) long. It was almost six feet (two meters) high. The Jeep was just over five feet (one and one-half meters) wide. It was powered by a small gasoline engine. The Jeep's top speed was about 65 miles (104 kilometers) per hour.

Jeeps were built by the Ford Motor Company and by Willys-Overland. Almost 660,000 Jeeps were built during World War II.

The All-Around Truck

With its four powered wheels, the Jeep could go almost anywhere. Jeeps could climb hills and drive through swamps. But on roads, Jeeps rolled over easily if a driver turned a corner too sharply. Drivers had to be careful.

The Jeep was used as everything from a scout vehicle to a tractor. As a scout vehicle, it was used to spy on the enemy. As a tractor, it pulled equipment.

The Jeep is the most popular military truck ever.

The Jeep could carry troops up to the front lines. It was so small that it was not easily seen by enemy soldiers. It was so light that it could be carried in gliders. A glider is a special kind of aircraft without an engine. It cannot be heard by the enemy.

Some soldiers added armor plates to their Jeeps. Armor is anything used to protect vehicles, people, and cargo during combat. Armor is usually steel. But the Jeep was not designed for the extra weight of the armor. The weight caused serious mechanical problems.

This 6x6 cargo truck was called a Jimmy.

The 6x6 Cargo Truck

Almost 600,000 6x6 cargo trucks were built during World War II. There were more 6x6 cargo trucks in service than any other kind of wartime vehicle. The 6x6 was built by the General Motors Corporation. U.S. soldiers called it the Jimmy.

The Jimmy could carry two and one-half tons (2.25 metric tons) of cargo or 12 seated

Jeeps were used in the Allied forces' D day assault.

soldiers. It could carry as many as 40 soldiers
if they were standing. There were many
versions of the Jimmy. They were used to carry
everything from horses to radar sets.

All Jimmys had gasoline engines. Their top
speed was 50 miles (80 kilometers) per hour.
With full fuel tanks, the trucks could travel 248
miles (397 kilometers). Many Jimmys were
armed with machine guns for protection.

D Day

On June 6, 1944, the U.S. Army landed on the
shores of France. This day is known as D day.
The Allied forces' D day mission was to push
the German troops out of France.

The United States belonged to the Allied
forces along with Great Britain, Canada, the
Soviet Union, and other countries. The Allied
forces fought together against Germany, Japan,
and Italy. In July 1944, Allied forces broke
through German lines.

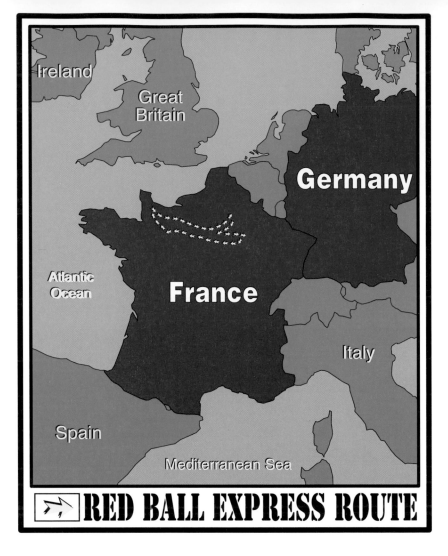

German military forces in France soon fell apart. They retreated back to Germany. But the Allied forces wanted to go after them before they reached home.

18

Jimmys in Action

After U.S. planes had destroyed all the French railroads, more than 5,000 Jimmys carried supplies to the Allied forces that were chasing the Germans. These trucks raced across France on special roads built by Allied engineers. The trucks ran nonstop, day and night. Only the dependable Jimmys could have kept running for so long.

The operation lasted 81 days. It became known as the Red Ball Express. The Jimmys kept the Allied tanks going until the railroads were fixed.

Tanks are enclosed vehicles protected with heavy armor. Tanks are mounted with various weapons, one of which is usually a large cannon. For extra traction, tanks move on tracks. Tracks are metal belts that run around wheels on both sides of a vehicle. The tanks that drove the German troops out of France owe a lot to the Jimmys that supplied them.

Chapter 3

Special U.S. Army Trucks

During World War II, the U.S. Army had problems unloading cargo from supply ships. The army wanted an amphibious (am-FIB-ee-us) truck. Amphibious means that a vehicle can operate both on land and in the water. The army decided to convert some of their 6x6 trucks into amphibious vehicles.

The army called this new vehicle the 6x6 Amphibian Truck. U.S. soldiers and sailors nicknamed it the Duck. More than 21,000 Ducks were built during World War II.

Amphibious vehicles are special trucks that operate both on land and in the water.

Duck Description

The Duck was a large vehicle. It was powered by a gasoline engine. One person could drive the Duck. But it normally had a crew of two.

The Duck had a watertight steel hull. The hull is the main body. If any water got into the vehicle, it was pushed out by three pumps.

A single large propeller moved the Duck through the water. This propeller was located at the rear of the vehicle. Top speed in the water was about six miles (10 kilometers) per hour.

Trucks that only carry tanks are called tank transporters.

On land, the Duck had six powered wheels. Its top speed was 45 miles (72 kilometers) per hour on flat ground. On rough or muddy ground, the Duck could not go as fast.

The Duck had no armor protection. It could be destroyed easily by the enemy.

Tank Transporters

Tanks break down when they are used a lot. To make tanks last longer, many armies carry them on large wheeled vehicles until the tanks are

The M26 was nicknamed the Dragon Wagon.

needed. These vehicles are called tank transporters.

To keep up with German tank designs, the United States made bigger and heavier tanks. The U.S. Army needed a vehicle designed especially for hauling the large tanks.

The M26
The U.S. Army designed a large tractor that weighed 12 tons (11 metric tons). This tractor

was known as the M26. A tractor is any truck
designed to pull a trailer. The M26 towed a
long trailer that could carry the army's
heaviest tanks.

The M26 was nicknamed the Dragon
Wagon. Early models had armor protection.
Later models did not have the armor. The
crew was armed with a single machine gun.
Almost 1,400 of these vehicles were built
during World War II.

Chapter 4

Postwar U.S. Army Trucks

The U.S. Army bought new 6x6 trucks after World War II. The trucks were nicknamed the Eager Beavers. They could carry two and one-half tons (2.25 metric tons) of cargo. The Eager Beavers replaced the army's World War II trucks.

The army developed a special 6x6 truck to carry heavier loads. It was known as the M54. The M54 could carry five tons (4.5 metric tons) of cargo. The M54 had a gasoline engine.

The 6x6 Eager Beavers replaced the U.S. Army's World War II trucks.

The M809 was the first U.S. Army truck to burn diesel fuel instead of gasoline.

The 1970s

In the 1970s, the army bought the M809 truck. The M809 truck could carry five tons (4.5 metric tons) of cargo. Instead of a gasoline engine, it had a diesel engine.

Diesel is a fuel similar to gasoline. Diesel engines are more powerful and more reliable than gasoline engines. They also travel more miles per gallon (more kilometers per liter) of fuel. Diesel fuel is also less likely to explode if struck by a mine or enemy fire.

The 1980s

In the early 1980s, the U.S. Army bought a new truck. It was called the M939. It had an automatic transmission. A transmission shifts a vehicle's gears. Automatic transmissions are easier to operate than manual transmissions. Manual transmissions need to be shifted by hand.

A winch was mounted on the front of the M939. A winch is a small electric motor connected to a long chain or cable. The chain or cable has a hook at the end of it. If the M939 truck gets stuck, the winch can pull it out.

The M939 truck came in different versions. Each version performed a different job. There were M939 fuel trucks, cargo trucks, dump trucks, tow trucks, and repair trucks. The M939 truck normally carried five tons (4.5 metric tons) of cargo.

The HEMTT is an 8x8 truck that comes in five versions.

The U.S. Army still has 40,000 of the
M939-type trucks in service.

Eight-Wheeled Trucks

Another modern truck is the Heavy Expanded
Mobility Tactical Truck. This truck is called
HEMTT for short. It is an 8x8. The HEMTT
can carry up to 11 tons (10 metric tons) of
cargo.

There are five different types of HEMTTs in
service. These include a fuel truck, a tow truck,
and two types of cargo carriers. Cargo carriers

are vehicles that carry supplies and ammunition. The fifth type of HEMTT is used to pull a trailer that launches a missile.

The U.S. Army has about 12,000 HEMTTs in service. All models of the HEMTT have powerful diesel engines. The diesel engine is connected to an automatic transmission. The HEMTT can go 330 miles (528 kilometers) on a full tank of fuel. The top speed of the vehicle is 50 miles (80 kilometers) per hour.

Postwar Tank Transporters

In the 1950s, the U.S. Army replaced the M26 with the M123 tank transporter. The new M123 was powered by a large diesel engine. The M123 could pull a trailer with a tank weighing 55 tons (50 metric tons).

U.S. Army tanks have grown in size and weight since the 1950s. The U.S. Army now has tanks that weigh more than 72 tons (65 metric tons). Because of the heavy tanks, the army was forced to buy an even larger tank transporter.

The M1070 HET

The M1070 HET is the newest tank transporter. HET stands for Heavy Equipment Transporter. The HET is an 8x8 vehicle. The tractor alone is more than 30 feet (10 meters) long. It takes a lot of skill to drive such a long vehicle.

The HET has a powerful diesel engine. The engine is connected to an automatic transmission.

The HET can carry the army's biggest tanks. The tanks do not ride on the tractor with the driver. Instead, the tank rides on a 20-wheel trailer that is towed behind the HET tractor.

Wartime Use of the HET

The U.S. Army used HETs during the Persian Gulf War in 1991. This war was fought by the United States and other United Nations countries, including Great Britain, Egypt (EE-jipt), France, and Saudi Arabia (SOW-dee uh-RAY-be-uh). They fought against Iraq (eye-RACK), which had invaded Kuwait (koo-WAIT). The Persian Gulf War is also known as Operation Desert Storm.

The HET truck was used during the Persian Gulf War.

The Persian Gulf is in the Middle East. There are few railroads in the Middle East. HETs were crucial to the army supply system. HETs were able to carry their loads over long distances very quickly.

Chapter 5

Safer Army Trucks

The Jeep is no longer used by the U.S. Army. It was replaced by the Hummer. The Hummer is a powerful, lightweight 4x4.

The Hummer has a diesel engine. It can carry more than one ton (one metric ton) of cargo or weapons. Its top speed is 65 miles (104 kilometers) per hour on highways. On rough terrain, the Hummer can go 30 miles (48 kilometers) per hour.

The Hummer comes in many different versions. More than 100,000 Hummers have been built for the military.

The 4x4 Hummer replaced the U.S. Army's Jeep.

The Hummer

Fiberglass Hood

Winch

Off-Road Tires

Hummers are used for many tasks. This one has been modified into an ambulance.

The Hummer

Because the Hummer is so wide, it does not roll over very easily. This makes the Hummer a safe vehicle to operate. Hummers also have a roll bar that protects the driver and any riders in case of an accident. A roll bar is made of strong metal tubes welded together. The roll bar crosses over the heads of the people in the vehicle.

The Hummer's frame is made of steel. The hood is fiberglass. Fiberglass is a strong, lightweight material. The body is made of aluminum. Aluminum is a lightweight metal alloy. An alloy is mixture of two or more metals. Aluminum is used to build cars, airplanes, tanks, and many other things that can benefit from less weight.

The Hummer is held together with rivets and glue. A rivet is a small metal bolt that is permanently fastened once it is squeezed together.

The basic Hummer has no armor. Some versions have thin armor protection. Many Hummers were used during the Persian Gulf War. They were equipped with several kinds of weapons.

Hummer Weapons

The Hummer can carry the TOW antitank missile system. TOW stands for Tubed Optically Wire-guided missile. The TOW missile has an armor-piercing warhead. This warhead can burn a hole through the thickest tank armor.

Many Hummers carry a machine gun that fires small grenades. This weapon is known as the Mark 19. It fires up to six grenades per second. It is deadly against enemy soldiers in open fields.

The Hummer can also carry missiles to protect against attacks from helicopters and planes. These missiles are called Stingers. They are attracted to the heat of aircraft engines. Once fired, they fly into a plane's engine and blow it up. The Hummer with the Stinger missiles is called the Avenger.

The FMTV and the Future

The U.S. Army's newest types of trucks are known as the Family of Medium Tactical Vehicles (FMTVs). FMTVs come in 15 different versions.

FMTVs can operate at high speeds on highways. They can also be used on the

The FMTVs come in 15 different versions.

roughest roads. FMTVs can cross thick mud or soft sand easily.

FMTVs are the latest in a long line of army trucks. The military trucks of the future may change in shape and size, but the important job they perform will remain the same.

Words to Know

aluminum (uh-LOO-mi-nuhm)—a lightweight metal alloy

armor (AR-mur)—anything used to protect vehicles, people, and cargo during combat

cargo carrier (KAR-goh KA-ree-ur)—a vehicle used for carrying supplies and ammunition

D day (DEE DAY)—June 6, 1944, when Allied forces landed on the northern shores of France to push the German military out

diesel engine (DEE-zuhl EN-juhn)—an engine that burns diesel fuel rather than gasoline

Hummer (HUM-ur)—a powerful, lightweight, diesel-powered 4x4 truck that replaced the Jeep

Jeep (JEEP)—a small, popular, gasoline-powered 4x4 truck used for multiple purposes by the U.S. Army. After World War II, Jeeps were also made for civilians.

Jimmy (JIM-ee)—a gasoline-powered 6x6 cargo truck built by the General Motors Corporation

Persian Gulf War (PER-zjun GULF WOR)—a war fought by the United States and other United Nations countries against Iraq in 1991; also known as Operation Desert Storm

Stinger (STING-ur)—antiaircraft missiles that protect people and vehicles on the land against attacks from helicopters and planes

tank (TANGK)—enclosed vehicle protected with heavy armor

TOW (TOH)—an antitank missile system with an armor-piercing warhead

tracks (TRAKS)—metal belts that run around wheels on both sides of a vehicle

To Learn More

Church, John. *Military Vehicles of World War II*. New York: Crescent Books, 1982.

Crismon, Fred W. *U.S. Military Wheeled Vehicles*. Sarasota, Fla.: Crestline Publications, 1983.

Foss, Christopher F. *Military Vehicles of the World*. New York: Charles Scribner's Sons, 1976.

Foss, Christopher F. *Modern Military Trucks*. London: Jane's Publishing Company, 1981.

Georgano, G.N. *World War II Military Vehicles*. London: Osprey Automotive, 1994.

Smith, Jay H. *Humvees and Other Military Vehicles*. Minneapolis: Capstone Press, 1995.

Useful
Addresses

AM General Corporation
105 North Niles Avenue
P.O. Box 7025
South Bend, IN 46634-7025

Oshkosh Truck Corporation
P.O. Box 2566
Oshkosh, WI 54903

U.S. Army Transportation Museum
Building 300 (Besson Hall)
Fort Eustic, VA 23604-5260

Virginia Museum of Military Vehicles
Aden Field
Nokesville, VA 22123

Internet Sites

Toyland Combat Vehicles
http://www.phoenix.net/~toyland/vehicles.htm

U.S. Army Transportation Corps
http://www.eustis.army.mil

World War I—Another Look
http://amug.org/~avishari/WWIp2.html

World War II Stories
http://www.islandnet.com/~awong/war/
index.html

This military truck was used in an assault by the 4th
Battalion during the Persian Gulf War.

Index

Allied forces, 17-19
alloy, 39
aluminum, 39
amphibious, 21
armor, 14, 19, 23, 25, 39, 40
Avenger, 40

Canada, 18

D day, 17
Dragon Wagon, 25
Duck, 21-23

Eager Beaver, 27
Egypt, 32

fiberglass, 39
FMTV, 40, 41
France, 17-19

General Motors Corporation, 16
General Purpose vehicle, 9
German, 17-19, 24
Great Britain, 18, 32

HEMTT, 30-31
Hummer, 35, 38-40

Iraq, 32
Italy, 18

Japan, 18
Jeep, 8, 9, 11, 13, 14, 35
Jimmy, 16, 17, 19

Mark 19, 40
M809, 28
M54, 27
Middle East, 33
M939, 29, 30
M1070 HET, 32, 33
M123, 31
M26, 25, 31

Operation Desert Storm, 32

Persian Gulf War, 32, 39

Red Ball Express, 19

Saudi Arabia, 32
6x6 cargo truck, 15
Soviet Union, 18
Stinger, 40

tank, 17, 19, 23-25, 31, 32, 39, 40
tank transporter, 23, 24, 31, 32
TOW, 39

United States, 11, 18, 24, 32
U.S. Army, 8, 9, 11, 17, 21, 24, 25,
    27-32, 35, 40
U.S. Marine Corps, 11

Willys, 9
Willys-Overland, 13
World War II, 11, 13, 15, 21, 27